Pirate Adventures!

Paul Mason

Published 2011 by
A&C Black Publishers Ltd.
36 Soho Square, London, W1D 3QY

www.acblack.com

ISBN   HB 978-1-4081-3369-9
       PB 978-1-4081-3368-2

Text copyright © 2010 Paul Mason

This book is produced using paper that is made from wood grown in managed, sustainable
forests. It is natural, renewable and recyclable. The logging and manufacturing processes
conform to the environmental regulations of the country of origin.

Produced for A&C Black by Calcium. www.calciumcreative.co.uk

Printed and bound in China by C&C Offset Printing Co.

Acknowledgements

The publishers would like to thank the following for their kind permission to reproduce
their photographs:

Cover: Shutterstock
Pages: Corbis: Bettmann 18, Christie's Images 9, Lebrecht Music & Arts 14, 20; Shutterstock:
Argus 15, Galina Barskaya 8, Cbpix 7, Bobby Deal/RealDealPhoto 4, J. Helgason 1, 19, IlFede
10, Ingrids 17, Kruglov_Orda 21, SeDmi 12, Maksim Shmeljov 3, 6, James Steidl 16, Robb
Williams 5, Xiver 11; Wikipedia: Howard Pyle 13.

Contents

Pirates Ahoy!

Long ago, **pirates** sailed the seas and **oceans** all over the world. They stole treasure and ships.

Tough fighters

Pirates were very fierce. Anyone who would not **surrender** to them without a fight could be killed.

Pirates fought with many **weapons**.

Pirate flag

Pirate flags were usually black with a white picture. This one is called the Jolly Roger.

Show me the treasure!

Indian Treasure

Pirate **Captain** Henry Avery is most famous for **capturing** the Indian treasure ship, *Gang-I-Sawai*. It was packed with gold, silver, and jewels.

Where did it go?

Soon after capturing the treasure ship, Avery disappeared. No one is sure where he or his treasure went.

The ship was full of treasure chests.

Pirate or shark?

Some sailors on the ship jumped into the shark-filled sea rather than fight the pirates!

So much treasure

Pirate Brothers

The **Mediterranean Sea** was sailed by lots of pirates. The Barbarossa brothers, Aruj and Kheir-ed-Din, were the scariest.

Don't get caught!
Kheir-ed-Din attacked ships and towns. The people he caught were often made **slaves**.

No ship was safe from the brothers.

Ginger beards

The brothers were given the nickname 'Barbarossa' meaning 'Red Beard', because they often dyed their beards red.

Call me Red Beard!

The Kindest Pirate

Not all pirate captains were fierce and frightening. Edward England was famous for being kind to his prisoners!

Clear off!

In fact, England was so nice that his crew got fed up with him and left him on an island! He escaped in a small boat, and decided to stop being a pirate.

Imagine being left on a desert island!

Is anyone there?

Flag of fear

At least Edward's pirate flag was scary. It was a human skull with two leg bones.

Kidd's Treasure

What did pirates do with their treasure? Many buried it. The most famous buried treasure belonged to William Kidd.

Lost forever?

Kidd is said to have buried lots of treasure along the east coast of the USA. No one has found any – yet!

Where is Kidd's treasure?

Pirates also called their treasure 'booty'.

William Kidd

Deadly secret

Stories say Kidd killed the people who buried his treasure, so no one but Kidd knew where it was.

Murad Rais

Jan Janz was a **Dutch** captain who became a pirate. He then changed his name to Murad Rais.

Slave catcher

Rais became a famous pirate. One of his most **daring raids** was in Iceland. Rais caught 400 people to be sold as slaves.

Save me!

Rais's prisoners beg for their lives.

Fly the flag

Murad Rais flew the moon and star flag.

Murad Rais

The Best Pirate

Bartholomew Roberts was a pirate captain for just four years. Yet he was the most **successful** pirate ever!

Dying young

Roberts once said that, "A merry life and a short one shall be my **motto**." His motto came true. He died in a battle aged 40.

Roberts captured over 400 ships!

Rum or tea?

Most pirates loved drinking rum, yet Roberts drank only tea!

Sail away!

Scariest Pirate

The scariest pirate was Edward Teach, known as 'Blackbeard'. His **victims** were often so scared, they did not put up a fight!

Bang, you're dead!

Blackbeard's crew was terrified of him too. It was probably because he sometimes used to shoot them – for no reason!

Blackbeard

Blackbeard in his very last fight.

I'm on fire!

Blackbeard used to put burning fuses into his hair and beard to make himself look like a devil.

Are you scared?

Women Pirates

On many pirate ships, the punishment for bringing a woman on board was death! Even so, a few women did become pirates.

We'll fight you!

Anne Bonny and Mary Read were both pirates. They were famous for being fiercer fighters than the men.

Anne Bonny

Who are you calling a girl?

Choose a weapon

Pirates fought with guns called pistols and muskets. They also used swords called cutlasses.

Anne Bonny and Mary Read were deadly fighters.

Mary Read

Glossary

captain person in charge of a ship and its sailors

capturing taking prisoner

daring fearless

desert island island where no one lives

Dutch person from a country called the Netherlands

flags pieces of material with a picture or a pattern

Mediterranean Sea sea between southern Europe and North Africa

motto rule or saying which someone lives by

oceans huge areas of saltwater

pirates sailors who stole ships and their treasure

raids attacks

slaves people forced to work for no pay

successful very good at something

surrender to give in

victims people killed or hurt by someone

weapons tools, such as guns and swords, used to fight

Further Reading

Websites

Examine the Pirates Fact File and find out if pirates really made their victims walk the plank at:
www.nmm.ac.uk/explore/sea-and-ships/pirates

Find out more about the most famous pirates and read a glossary of pirate words at:
www.thepiratesrealm.com

Books

How To Be A Pirate In 10 Easy Stages by Scoular Anderson, Collins Educational (2004).

Pirates (True Stories and Legends) by Jim Pipe, Franklin Watts (2009).

See Inside Pirate Ships by Rob Lloyd Jones, Usborne (2007).

Index